WALKING IN VICTORY AND AUTHORITY OF THE TRUTH

"And ye shall know the truth, and the truth shall make you free."

John 8:32

By
Franklin N. Abazie

Walking in Victory and Authority of the Truth

COPYRIGHT 2018 BY Franklin N Abazie
ISBN: 978:0-9966-263-7-8
All right reserved. This book or any portion thereof may not be reproduced or used in any manner whatsoever without the express written permission of the publisher, except for the use of brief quotations in a book review. All Bible quotes are from King James Version and others as noted.

Published by: F N ABAZIE PUBLISHING HOUSE---
a.k.a,
Empowerment Bookstore:

That I may publish with the voice of thanksgiving and tell of all thy wondrous works. **Psalms26:7**

To order additional copies, wholesales or booking: Call the Church office (973-372-7518)
or Empowerment Bookstore Hotline 973-393-8518
Worship address:
343 Sanford Avenue Newark New Jersey 07106
Administrative Head Office address:
33 Schley Street Newark New Jersey 07112
Email:pastorfranknto@yahoo.com
Website www.fnabaziehealingministries.org
Publishing House: www.fnabaziepublishinghouse.org

This book is a production of F N Abazie Publishing House.

A publication Arms of Miracle of God Ministries 2018
First Edition

CONTENTS

THE MANDATE OF THE COMMISSION...........iv

ARMS OF THE COMMISSION............................v

INTRODUCTION..viii

CHAPTER 1

1. The Mind of Christ 50

CHAPTER 2

2. How do we walk by the Spirit?.........................65

CHAPTER 3

3. Prayer of Salvation..73

CHAPTER 4

4. About the Author...83

THE MANDATE OF THE COMMISSION

"THE MOMENT IS DUE TO IMPACT YOUR WORLD THROUGH THE REVIVAL OF THE HEALING & MIRACLE MINISTRY OF JESUS CHRIST OF NAZARETH.

I AM SENDING YOU TO RESTORE HEALTH UNTO THEE AND I WILL HEAL THEE OF THY WOUNDS, SAID THE LORD OF HOST."

ARMS OF THE COMMISSION

1) F N Abazie Ministries-Miracle of God Ministries (Miracle Chapel Intl)

2) F N Abazie TV Ministries: Global Television Ministry Outreach.

3) F N Abazie Radio Ministries: Radio Broadcasting Outreach.

4) F N Abazie Publishing House: Book Publication.

5) F N Abazie Bible School: also called Word of Healing Bible School (W.O.H.B.S)

6) F N Abazie Evangelistic Ass: Miracle of God Ministries: Global Crusade

7) Empowerment Bookstore: Book distribution.

8) F N Abazie Helping Hands: Meeting the help of the needy world wide

9) F N Abazie Disaster Recovery Mission: Global Disaster Recovery.

10) F N Abazie Prison Ministry: Prison Ministry for all convicts "Second chance"

Some of our ministry arms are waiting the appointed time to commence

FAVOR CONFESSION

Father thank you for making me righteous and accepted through the blood of Jesus Christ. Because of that, I am blessed and highly favored by God. I am the subject of your affection. Your favor surrounds me as a shield, and the first thing that people see around me is your favored shield.

Thank you that I have favor with you and man today. All day long people go out of their way to bless me and help me. I have favor with everyone that I deal with today. Doors that were once closed are now opened for me. I receive preferential treatment, and I have special privileges, I am Gods favored child.

No good thing will he withhold from me. Because of Gods favor my enemies cannot triumph over my life. I have supernatural increase and promotion. I declare restoration to everything that the devil has stolen from my life. I have honor in the midst of my adversaries and an increase in assets, especially in real estate and expansion of territories.

Because I am highly favored by God, I experience great victories, supernatural turnarounds, and miraculous breakthrough in the midst of great impossibilities. I receive recognition, prominence, and honor. Petitions are granted to me even by ungodly authorities. Policies, rules, regulations, and laws are changed and reverse on my behalf.

I win battles that I don't even have to fight, because God fights them for me. This is the day, the set time and the designated moment for me to experience the free favor of God, that profusely and lavishly abound on my behalf in Jesus name. Amen.

INTRODUCTION

"For we can do nothing against the truth, but for the truth."
2cor13:8

I may never meet with you in person. However, I am glad to meet with you here. I love the power of books in print. We are told that *the word of God is not bound.* In this small book, you will be excited to know more about walking in truth. There is power in humility and honesty.

"And ye shall know the truth, and the truth shall make you free." **John8:32**

"If the Son therefore shall make you free, ye shall be free indeed." **John8:36**

A lot of church folks do not tell the truth no matter the circumstance. This small book is designed to empower you to not only to be honest in life, but live by the truth. In my opinion, there is a question mark on our Christian life, if we have a character challenge. If we live a fake life of dishonesty.

David said So he fed them according to the integrity of his heart; and guided them by the skilfulness of his hands. If I may say this here, your skill and honesty go together in life.

The bible says *"Wealth gotten by vanity shall be diminished: but he that gathereth by labour shall increase."* **Proverb13:11**

It takes honesty, humility, and love for all to live a Godly life. If you must live for God the rest of your life. Come with me let's examine together what the Holy Spirit is saying concerning walking in victory and authority of the truth in life. I see you living for Jesus Christ.

Happy Reading!

HIS DESTINY WAS THE CROSS….

HIS PURPOSE WAS LOVE…..

HIS REASON WAS YOU….

"But if we walk in the light, as he is in the light, we have fellowship one with another, and the blood of Jesus Christ his Son cleanseth us from all sin."

1 John 1:7

"The lips of the righteous know what is acceptable: but the mouth of the wicked speaketh frowardness."

Proverb10:32

"Then said Jesus to those Jews which believed on him, If ye continue in my word, then are ye my disciples indeed."

John8:31

"And ye shall know the truth, and the truth shall make you free."

John8:32

"For we can do nothing against the truth, but for the truth."

2cor13:8

"Lead me in thy truth, and teach me: for thou art the God of my salvation; on thee do I wait all the day."

Psalms25:5

"Thy word have I hid in mine heart, that I might not sin against thee."

Psalms 119:11

"I have no greater joy than to hear that my children walk in truth."

3John1:4

"But speaking the truth in love, may grow up into him in all things, which is the head, even Christ."

Ephesians4:15

"In whom we have redemption through his blood, even the forgiveness of sins:"

Col1:14

" The sum of your word is truth, and every one of your righteous rules endures forever."

Psalm 119:160

"But I will tell you what is inscribed in the book of truth: there is none who contends by my side against these except Michael, your prince."

Daniel 10:21

"Sanctify them in the truth; your word is truth."

John17:17

"In him you also, when you heard the word of truth, the gospel of your salvation, and believed in him, were sealed with the promised Holy Spirit, who is the guarantee of our inheritance until we acquire possession of it, to the praise of his glory."

Ephesians1:13-14

"Of his own will he brought us forth by the word of truth, that we should be a kind of firstfruits of his creatures."

James1:18

"Of a truth, God will not do wickedly, and the Almighty will not pervert justice."

Job 34:12

"Lead me in your truth and teach me,
for you are the God of my salvation;
for you I wait all the day long."

Psalms25:5

"Send out your light and your truth; let them lead me; let them bring me to your holy hill and to your dwelling"

Psalms 43:3

"Teach me your way, O LORD, that I may walk in your truth; unite my heart to fear your name."

Psalms86:11

Prayer Points

Every power assigned to follow me, to destroy me, die in the Name of Jesus.

Therefore, let our enemies be delivered into the hands of their enemies in Jesus name!

It is written; *"You shall be for fuel of fire; your blood shall be in the midst of the land. You shall not be remembered, for I the Lord have spoken"* (**Ezekiel. 21:32**)

Therefore, let all our spiritual enemies become fuel for divine fire in Jesus name!

It is written; *"Then they will know that I am the Lord, when I have set a fire in Egypt and all her helpers are destroyed"* (**Ezekiel. 30:8**).

Therefore, O Lord, let all the helpers of our enemies be destroyed in the name of Jesus.

It is written; *"And the people to whom they prophesy shall be cast out in the streets of Jerusalem because of the famine and the sword; they will have no one to bury them nor their wives, their sons nor their daughters – for I will pour their wickedness on them"* (**Jer. 14:16**).

Therefore, O Lord, pour the wickedness of those who seek to destroy us upon their own heads in the name of Jesus!

It is written; *"Call together the archers against Babylon. All you who bend the bow encamp against it all around; let none of them escape. Repay her according to her work; According to all she has done, do to her; for she has been poured against the Lord, against the Holy one of Israel"* (**Jer. 50:29**).

Therefore, let all the hosts of the Lord turn against our spiritual enemies in Jesus name!

It is written; *"Let God arise, let His enemies be scattered; let those also who hate him flee before him"* (**Psalms. 68:1**).

Therefore, O God, arise and let all your enemies in our lives be scattered in Jesus name!

It is written; *"And He that searches the hearts knows what the mind of the spirit is, because He makes intercession for the saints according to the will of God."* (**Romans 8:27**)

Therefore, the intercessory prayers of Jesus, who is seated on the right hand of the throne of God, will not be in vain over our lives, in the name of Jesus.

It is written; *"The Lord is your keeper; the Lord is the shade at your right hand."*

The sun shall not strike you by day, nor the moon by night. The Lord shall preserve you from all evil; He shall preserve your soul.

The Lord shall preserve our going out and our coming in from this time forth, and even forevermore (Psalms. 121:5-8)

Therefore, O Lord, spread your covering of fire and the blood of Jesus over us and our loved ones, in the name of Jesus.

It is written; *"Rejoice always, pray without ceasing, in everything give thanks; for this is the will of God in Christ Jesus for you."* (**1 Thess. 5:16:18**).

Therefore, we thank you Father, for raising a spiritual shield over our loved ones and us.

Thank you for giving us the heart for appreciating everything you are doing for us.

Thank you for filling our hearts and our home with joy and peace that surpasses all understanding. Blessed be your name for all the answers to our prayers in the name of Jesus!

You are holy, holy, Lord God Almighty, who was and is and is to come, Amen!

O Lord, let our season of divine intervention appear in the name of Jesus!

O you gates in the heavenlies standing against our destiny, lift up your heads in the name of Jesus!

O you gates in the waters standing against our destiny, lift up your heads in the name of Jesus!

O you gates in the earth standing against our destiny, lift up your heads in the name of Jesus!

O you gates under the earth standing against our destiny, lift up your heads in the name of Jesus!

O God, arise and destroy every gate keeper assigned against our lives in the name of Jesus!

We break the backbone of every spirit of scarcity in our lives in the name of Jesus!

O Lord anoint our eyes to see divine opportunities in the name of Jesus!

Lord let every blindness to the treasures of our lives be cleared in the name of Jesus!

Let our divine helpers appear in the name of Jesus!

We declare, O Lord, that the rest of our lives will be better than the first part, in Jesus name!

We declare, O Lord that will overcome obstacles and defeat every enemy, in Jesus name!

We declare, O Lord that every blessing and promise that you put in our hearts will come to pass because this is our time for favor, in Jesus name!

We declare, O Lord that this is a new season of increase in our lives. We speak health, wisdom, creativity, divine connections, and supernatural opportunities. They are coming our way, in Jesus name!

We declare, O Lord that we choose faith over fear. We are victorious in faith, in Jesus name!

We declare, O Lord that that we are not just surviving, this is our time to thrive in prosperity, in Jesus name!

We declare, O Lord that we will believe that we have received in the spirit even though we do not see anything happening in the flesh, in Jesus name!

We declare, O Lord that our rewards are being transferred to us because we remain in faith, in Jesus name!

We declare, O Lord that doubt will not ruin our optimistic spirit, in Jesus name!

We declare, O Lord that we are prisoners of hope and get up every morning expecting your favor, in Jesus name!

We declare, O Lord that you will do amazing things in our lives, in Jesus name!

We declare, O Lord that we are closer to your abundant blessing than we think, our time has come, your promises will come to pass, in Jesus name!

We declare, O Lord that we will stay in an attitude of faith and expectation, in Jesus name!

We declare, O Lord that we are not worried, we know that you are our vindicator. It may seem to be taking a long time, but we will reap in due season if trust in you Lord, in Jesus name!

We declare, O Lord that you know the secret petitions our heart and we believe that they will come to fulfilment, in Jesus name!

We declare, O Lord that you will open new doors for us, in Jesus name!

We declare, O Lord that we will see your goodness, in Jesus name!

We declare, O Lord that this is our time to believe because favor is coming our way, in Jesus name!

We declare, O Lord that you have paved the way to abundant prosperity for us, prosperity more than we can every dream of or imagine, for your sake, in Jesus name!

We declare, O Lord that in your eyes our future is extremely bright, in Jesus name!

We declare, O Lord that we will rise higher and higher and see more of your favor and blessings and we will live the prosperous life you have in store for us, in Jesus name!

We declare, O Lord that we may have a lot of turmoil, but we know that everything is going to be alright, in Jesus name!

We declare, O Lord that we have faith because we have put you first, in Jesus name!

We thank you, O Lord that our set time for favor is here, in Jesus name!

We declare, O Lord that our hour of deliverance has come, in Jesus name!

We declare, O Lord that there is no limit to what we can do, in Jesus name!

We declare, O Lord that there is no obstacle we cannot overcome, in Jesus name!

We declare, O Lord that that we have seen your accomplishments and they are good, in Jesus name!

We declare, O Lord that there is no challenge that is too great for us because you are with us, in Jesus name!

We declare, O Lord that you always succeed, in Jesus name!

We declare, O Lord that there is no financial difficulty or situation in our lives that is too great for you to resolve, in Jesus name!

We declare, O Lord that you are our Father Jehovah Jireh and that you own everything and you are our provider, in Jesus name!

We declare, O Lord that your promises declare that we are destined to live a victorious life, in Jesus name!

We declare, O Lord that we are your children, in Jesus name!

We declare, O Lord that the seeds of increase, success, and promotion are taking a new root; your favor will spring forth in our lives in a great way; we will see new seasons of blessings and new seasons of your favor. It's our time to have abundant faith, in Jesus name!

O Lord, it is written; *"According to your faith, it will be done unto you."* **Ps. 2:8** says *"ask me and I will give you the nations as your inheritance."*

Therefore, we ask you Lord to fulfil our highest hopes and dreams, in Jesus name!

We ask you this day, O Lord to give us our abundant blessing now, in Jesus name!

We dare to exercise our faith by asking you O Lord so that we may receive indeed, in Jesus name!

We thank you O Lord that for encouraging our faith, in Jesus name!

We declare, O Lord that this is our time for favor, in Jesus name!

We declare, O Lord that this is our time to prosper abundantly, in Jesus name!

We declare, O Lord that this is our time to have instant answers to prayer, in Jesus name!

We declare, O Lord that this is our time to ask and receive, in Jesus name!

We declare, O Lord that this is our time to thank you and testify for answered prayer, in Jesus name!

We declare, O Lord that we are blessed and that goodness and mercy are following us right now, in Jesus name!

We declare, O Lord that you favor is surrounding us like a shield – you prosper us even in the desert, in Jesus name!

We declare, O Lord that you have great things for us in the spirit and that you have already released favor into our prayers, in Jesus name!

We declare, O Lord that you are a great and Holy God, in Jesus name!

It is written; *"Delight yourself in the Lord and he will give you the desires of your heart."* (**Ps 37:4**).

We therefore declare, O Lord that we delight in you because you are our Father God and because we are your children you have made us the head and not the tail.

We declare, O Lord that because we are your children, we are more than conquerors, in Jesus name!

We declare, O Lord that we are blessed and you supply all our needs. We have more than enough, in Jesus name!

We declare, O Lord that we have abundant favor indeed, in Jesus name!

We declare, O Lord that we are filled indeed with the presence of the Holy Spirit, in Jesus name!

We declare, O Lord that we have abundant faith indeed, in Jesus name!

We declare, O Lord that you have answered our prayers, in Jesus name!

We declare, O Lord that our debts are all paid up, in Jesus name!

We declare, O Lord that we are healthy, in Jesus name!

We declare, O Lord that we have no lack and that we have more than enough, in Jesus name!

We declare, O Lord that we are extremely blessed so much that we can bless your kingdom, in Jesus name!

We declare, O Lord that we are extremely blessed so much that we can bless others, in Jesus name!

We declare, O Lord that we have entered into an anointing of ease, in Jesus name!

We declare, O Lord that for every opportunity we have missed, every chance we've blown, you will turn the clock and bring bigger and better things across our path, in Jesus name!

We declare, O Lord that we will not settle for less than your best, in Jesus name!

Please restore the time that we have lost, O Lord that, in Jesus name!

Restore our victories, O Lord, in Jesus name!

Restore our lost joy, lost peace, lost health, lost insight, lost faith, lost dedication, and desire to please you, we declare, O Lord in Jesus name!

We declare, O Lord that you use what was meant for our harm to our advantage, in Jesus name!

We declare, O Lord that you are a faithful God, in Jesus name!

We declare, O Lord that you will blossom our lives in ways that we can never imagine, in Jesus name!

We know, O Lord that you will bless us abundantly, in Jesus name!

We know, O Lord that you will provide divine connections, in Jesus name!

We declare, O Lord that we are not suffering – we are blessed, in Jesus name!

We declare, O Lord that our difficulties will give way to new growth, new opportunities, and new vision, in Jesus name!

O Lord let us see your blessing bloom in our lives in ways we would never dreamt possible, in Jesus name!

We declare, O Lord that we will stay in faith, so that what was meant to stop us will not be a stumbling block but a stepping stone taking us to a higher level, in Jesus name!

We declare, O Lord that we are not ordinary, but we are children of the most high God, in Jesus name!

We declare, O Lord that we created to rise above problems, in Jesus name!

We declare victory over strife O Lord, in Jesus name!

We declare, O Lord that no weapon formed against us shall prosper, in Jesus name!

We declare, O Lord that we are healthy and that no sickness shall live in us, in Jesus name!

We declare, O Lord that triumph is our birthright, in Jesus name!

We declare, O Lord that our setbacks are simply setups for greater comebacks that will place us to be better than we were before, in Jesus name!

We declare, O Lord that with you all things are possible, in Jesus name!

We declare, O Lord that we are in agreement with you. We know you have supernatural favor in store for us. You have supernatural opportunities, supernatural healing, and supernatural restoration, in Jesus name!

We declare, O Lord that you want to do unusual things in our lives, in Jesus name!

We declare, O Lord that in faith, we have expectation deep in our spirits, in Jesus name!

We declare, O Lord that this will not be a survival year but a supernatural year in which you will abundantly come through for us, in Jesus name!

We believe, O Lord that you have come through for us, in Jesus name!

We declare, O Lord that because we hope in you, we will not be put to shame, in Jesus name!

We declare, O Lord that your word is right and true, you are faithful in all you do, in Jesus name!

We declare, O Lord that you are our refuge and strength, an ever present helper, in Jesus name!

We declare, O Lord that we will cast our cares on you and you will sustain us, you will never let the righteous fall, in Jesus name!

We declare, O Lord that you are the strength of our hearts and our portion forever, in Jesus name!

We declare, O Lord that you are our dwelling, therefore, no harm will befall us, and no disaster will come near our tent, in Jesus name!

We declare, O Lord that you are our refuge and our fortress, in Jesus name!

We declare, O Lord that you will command your angels concerning us to guard us in all our ways, in Jesus name!

We declare, O Lord that even in darkness the light will dawn for us, in Jesus name!

We declare, O Lord that your word is eternal and stands firm in the heavens, in Jesus name!

We declare, O Lord that your faithfulness will continue throughout all generations, in Jesus name!

We declare, O Lord that you will keep us from harm; you will watch over our lives; you will watch over our coming and our going both now and for evermore, in Jesus name! (**Ps. 121**)

Thank you O Lord for the assurance that you are watching over us even when we sleep, in Jesus name! (**Ps. 13:5-6**)

We declare, O Lord that you will drive those that do evil away from us and that you will protect us from their influence, in Jesus name! (**Ps. 66:1-4**)

We will shout with joy to you O Lord, we will sing the glory of your name and make your praise glorious. How awesome are your deeds! So great is your power that your enemies cringe before you, in Jesus name!

We declare, O Lord that that we will give you thanks for you answered us, in Jesus name! (**Ps. 118:21**)

We declare, O Lord that we will praise you with all our hearts; before the gods we will sing your praise. We will bow down towards your Holy temple and will praise your name for your love and your faithfulness, for you have exalted above all things, your name and your word, in Jesus name! (**Ps. 138:1-3**)

Amen.

CHAPTER 1
The Mind of Christ

"For who hath known the mind of the Lord, that he may instruct him? but we have the mind of Christ." **1cor2:16**

The Mind of Christ is the mind of victory. *The mind of Christ is the mind of Christ is the mind of the overcomer.* Like I preach all the time, our mind must be renewed daily if we must have *the mind of Christ.*

It is written *"And be not conformed to this world: but be ye transformed by the renewing of your mind, that ye may prove what is that good, and acceptable, and perfect, will of God."* **Romans12:2**

For unless we transform our mindset into the mind of Jesus Christ we will never be able to endure persecution, trial, and tribulation in life.

Chapter 1 - The Mind of Christ

It is written *"These things I have spoken unto you, that in me ye might have peace. In the world ye shall have tribulation: but be of good cheer; I have overcome the world."* **John16:33**

What is the Mind of Christ?

The opening scripture said, *"For who has known the mind of the Lord that he may instruct him?' But we have the mind of Christ."* **1cor2:16**

The mind of Christ is the mind of faith and victory. The mind of victory is a winning spirit. We are told, *"For whatsoever is born of God overcometh the world: and this is the victory that overcometh the world, even our faith."* **1John5:4**

"Draw nigh to God, and he will draw nigh to you. Cleanse your hands, ye sinners; and purify your hearts, ye double minded." **James 4:8**

Jesus was never afraid nor intimidated to go to the cross.

Talking about Jesus, the word of God said,

"Let this mind be in you, which was also in Christ Jesus:"

"Who, being in the form of God, thought it not robbery to be equal with God:"

"But made himself of no reputation, and took upon him the form of a servant, and was made in the likeness of men:"

"And being found in fashion as a man, he humbled himself, and became obedient unto death, even the death of the cross."

Phil 2:5-8

In my opinion, every believer should have the Mind of Christ. The Mind of Christ is a hunger to seek the face of God in prayer. The Mind of Christ is a hunger to witness to unbelievers.

Chapter 1 - The Mind of Christ

"For the Son of Man came to seek and to save what was lost." Our approach to life and attitude should reflect that of Christ Jesus: *Who, being in the form of God, thought it not robbery to be equal with God."*

"But made himself of no reputation, and took upon him the form of a servant, and was made in the likeness of men:"

"And being found in fashion as a man, he humbled himself, and became obedient unto death, even the death of the cross."

The mind of Christ is to develop a loving and compassionate heart. *"And when the Lord saw her, he had compassion on her, and said unto her, Weep not."*

The mind of Christ is a heart of prayer. *"But Jesus often withdrew to lonely places and prayed."* The mind of Christ is the mind of the Holy Spirit. *"But God hath revealed them unto us by his Spirit: for the Spirit searcheth all things, yea, the deep things of God."*

"For what man knoweth the things of a man, save the spirit of man which is in him? even so the things of God knoweth no man, but the Spirit of God. Now we have received, not the spirit of the world, but the spirit which is of God; that we might know the things that are freely given to us of God." **1cor2:10-12**

Talking about the Holy Spirit Isaiah said….

"And the spirit of the Lord shall rest upon him, the spirit of wisdom and understanding, the spirit of counsel and might, the spirit of knowledge and of the fear of the Lord; And shall make him of quick understanding in the fear of the Lord: and he shall not judge after the sight of his eyes, neither reprove after the hearing of his ears:" **Isiah11:2-3**

The mind of Christ is a heart of faith. The mind of Christ is the mindset to succeed in life. The mind of Christ is boldness and authority to survive prevailing challenges and go through tough and difficult times. In this prevailing times, only those with the mind of Christ will make it big time.

Chapter 1 - The Mind of Christ

"But the path of the just is as the shining light, that shineth more and more unto the perfect day." **Proverb4:18**

"This book of the law shall not depart out of thy mouth; but thou shalt meditate therein day and night, that thou mayest observe to do according to all that is written therein: for then thou shalt make thy way prosperous, and then thou shalt have good success." **Joshua1:8**

The mind of Christ is to live an overcomer life. It is written, *"There hath no temptation taken you but such as is common to man: but God is faithful, who will not suffer you to be tempted above that ye are able; but will with the temptation also make a way to escape, that ye may be able to bear it."* **1cor10:13.**

"For whatsoever is born of God overcometh the world: and this is the victory that overcometh the world, even our faith." **1John5:4**

"Ye are of God, little children, and have overcome them: because greater is he that is in you, than he that is in the world." **1John4:4**

"And he said unto them, Ye are from beneath; I am from above: ye are of this world; I am not of this world." **John8:23**

"And he answered, Fear not: for they that be with us are more than they that be with them." **2King6:16**

HOW DO I WALK IN VICTORY AND AUTHORITY OF THE TRUTH

The truth is; whenever you are walking with someone together you won't be going in opposite directions. If you are in the opposite direction, then both of you are not together. *"Can two walk together, except they be agreed?"* **Amos3:3**

If you are walking in a different direction you cannot speak or pay attention to them, you can't enjoy them, you can't share things with them, and you won't be able to understand them.

Chapter 1 - The Mind of Christ

When you walk with the Lord Jesus, must comply to be in the perfect will of God for your life.

When you're constantly walking with someone you're going to understand them better than you ever did. You're going to know their heart. Walking with God is not just a time in the prayer closet, it's a lifestyle that we can only obtain through Jesus Christ.

".....but the people that do know their God shall be strong, and do exploits." **Daniel 11:32**

"Those who walk with God, always reach their destination." **Henry Ford**

"If I walk with the world, I can't walk with God." **Dwight L. Moody**

"God's mighty power comes when God's people learn to walk with God." **Jack Hyles**

"He has made it clear to you, mortal man, what is good and what the LORD is requiring from you— to act with justice, to treasure the LORD's gracious love, and to walk humbly in the company of your God." **Micah 6:8**

"So that you might live in a manner worthy of the Lord and be fully pleasing to him as you bear fruit while doing all kinds of good things and growing in the full knowledge of God. You are being strengthened with all power according to his glorious might, so that you might patiently endure everything with joy." **Colossians 1:10-11**

"Observe the commands of the LORD your God by walking in his ways and by fearing him." **Deut 8:6**

"Let us walk with decency, as in the daylight: not in carousing and drunkenness; not in sexual impurity and promiscuity; not in quarreling and jealousy." **Romans 13:13**

Chapter 1 - The Mind of Christ

"For we are His creation, created in Christ Jesus for good works, which God prepared ahead of time so that we should walk in them." **Ephesians 2:10**

"As for you, if you faithfully follow me as David your father did, obeying all my commands, decrees, and regulations, then I will establish the throne of your dynasty. For I made this covenant with your father, David, when I said, 'One of your descendants will always rule over Israel.'' **2 Chronicles 7:17-18**

"But he said to them, "I have food to eat that you know nothing about. Then his disciples said to each other, "Could someone have brought him food?" "My food," said Jesus, "is to do the will of him who sent me and to finish his work." **John 4:32-34**

"The one who says he resides in God ought himself to walk just as Jesus walked." **1 John 2:6**

When we walk with the Lord we draw closer to the Lord with all our heart. He becomes our focus. Our hearts longs for Him. Our heart seeks His presence. Our desire to have fellowship with Christ and be like Him will grow while our worldly desires will decrease.

"Let us continue to come near with sincere hearts in the full assurance that faith provides, because our hearts have been sprinkled clean from a guilty conscience, and our bodies have been washed with pure water." **Hebrews 10:22**

"Looking unto Jesus the author and finisher of our faith; who for the joy that was set before him endured the cross, despising the shame, and is set down at the right hand of the throne of God." **Hebrews 12:2**

"And he answering said, Thou shalt love the Lord thy God with all thy heart, and with all thy soul, and with all thy strength, and with all thy mind; and thy neighbour as thyself." **Luke 10:27**

Chapter 1 - The Mind of Christ

Whenever walking with God we desire to please God and we allow the Lord to work in our lives to make us into the image of His Son.

"Because those whom he foreknew he also predestined to be conformed to the image of his Son, that his Son would be the firstborn among many brothers and sisters." **Romans8:29**

"Being confident of this very thing, that he which hath begun a good work in you will perform it until the day of Jesus Christ." **Phil1:6**

When walking with the Lord you will grow in your awareness of sin in your life and your need for a Savior. More and more we will grow in hatred for our sins and want to rid our lives of them. More and more we will confess and forsake our sins.

"But the tax collector stood at a distance and would not even look up to heaven. Instead, he continued to beat his chest and said, 'O God, be merciful to me, the sinner that I am!" **Luke18:13**

"If we confess our sins, he is faithful and just and will forgive us our sins and purify us from all unrighteousness." **1John1:9**

When you're walking with God you don't let other things distract you from Christ.

"But Martha was distracted by her many tasks, and she came up and asked, "Lord, don't You care that my sister has left me to serve alone? So tell her to give me a hand." The Lord answered her, "Martha, Martha, you are worried and upset about many things, but one thing is necessary. Mary has made the right choice, and it will not be taken away from her." **Luke10:40-42**

We must walk by faith.

"Indeed, our lives are guided by faith, not by sight." **2cor5:7**

For in the gospel the righteousness of God is revealed—a righteousness that is by faith from first to last, just as it is written: *"The righteous will live by faith."* **Romans1:17**

Chapter 1 - The Mind of Christ

We can't walk with the Lord if we're living in darkness. You can't have God and evil.

"If we say we have fellowship with him and yet keep on walking in the darkness, we are lying and not practicing the truth. But if we walk in the light as he himself is in the light, we have fellowship with one another and the blood of Jesus his Son cleanses us from all sin." **1John1:6-7**

"I say then, walk by the Spirit and you will not carry out the desire of the flesh." **Gal5:16**

Your will must be aligned with God's will.

"Do two walk together unless they have agreed to do so?" **Amos3:3**

Enoch

"And Enoch walked with God after he begat Methuselah three hundred years, and begat sons and daughters:" **Genesis5:22**

Noah

Noah, however, found favor in the sight of the LORD. These are the family records of Noah. Noah was a righteous man, blameless among his contemporaries; Noah walked with God." Genesis6:8-9

Abraham

"He said to me, "The LORD before whom I have walked will send His angel with you and make your journey a success, and you will take a wife for my son from my family and from my father's household." **Genesis24:40**

"Jesus spoke to the people once more and said, "I am the light of the world. If you follow me, you won't have to walk in darkness, because you will have the light that leads to life." **John8:12**

CHAPTER 2
How do we Walk by the Spirit?

The phrase *"walking by the Spirit"* has been so must been interpreted that even the very elect like me and you are going astray of the sound doctrine of Christ Jesus. Judas Iscariot went his own way to betray Jesus Christ. The question is, was he walking in the spirit or in the flesh? Obvious we can conclude that he was in the flesh. But so many of us are doing the same thing today in different ways.

"This I say then, Walk in the Spirit, and ye shall not fulfil the lust of the flesh." **Gal5:16**

"If we live in the Spirit, let us also walk in the Spirit." **Gal5:25**

"For if ye live after the flesh, ye shall die: but if ye through the Spirit do mortify the deeds of the body, ye shall live." **Romans8:13**

I say all the time spiritual things are higher than physical things. Whenever we *"walk by the Spirit,"* we are walking in victory and in authority. We rule and dominate our world when we walk by the spirit of the living God. we are not controlled by our physical experience or fleshy nature.

Walking by the Spirit is what we do when the desires produced by the Spirit are stronger than the desires produced by the flesh. This means that "walking by the Spirit" is not something we do in order to get the Spirit's help, but rather, just as the phrase implies, it is something we do by the enablement of the Spirit.

Ultimately, the presence of the Holy Spirit help us conquer the wiles and schemes of the devil every time we walk in the spirit. Besides our spiritual nature we are mere flesh. *"And the Lord God formed man of the dust of the ground, and breathed into his nostrils the breath of life; and man became a living soul."*

Chapter 2 - How do we Walk by the Spirit?

"I know that in me, that is, in my flesh, dwells no good thing." **Romans 7:18**

Besides the powerful influences of the Holy Spirit, none of our inclinations or desires is holy or good, *"Because the carnal mind is enmity against God: for it is not subject to the law of God, neither indeed can be."* (**Romans 8:7**).

Contrary to any altar call you ever heard, you must be born again to receive the things of the spirit of God. Jesus answered, *"Verily, verily, I say unto thee, Except a man be born of water and of the Spirit, he cannot enter into the kingdom of God."* **John 3:5**

Brethren's you must be born again to *"walk by the Spirit"* is something the Holy Spirit enables us to do by producing in us strong desires that accord with God's will. This is what God said he would do in Ezekiel 36:26, 27:

"A new heart I will give you and a new spirit I will put within you . . . I will put my Spirit within you and cause you to walk in my statutes."

Thus when we *"walk by the Spirit,"* we experience the fulfillment of this prophecy. The Holy Spirit produces in us desires for God's way that are stronger than our fleshly desires, and thus he causes us to walk in God's statutes.

Works of the Flesh and Fruit of the Spirit

-----Confess your sins-----

We all know that Jesus is Lord. You have to take time to confess it with your mouth.

-----Pray-----

"And he spake a parable unto them to this end, that men ought always to pray, and not to faint;"

"Pray without ceasing."

-----Trust in the Lord-----

We are told *"They that trust in the Lord shall be as mount Zion, which cannot be removed, but abideth for ever."* **Psalms125:1**

Chapter 2 - How do we Walk by the Spirit?

-----Acknowledge the Lord in your life-----

For unless you acknowledge the Lord, he will not direct your path in life. *"In all thy ways acknowledge him, and he shall direct thy paths."* **Proverb3:6.**

"Because they regard not the works of the Lord, nor the operation of his hands, he shall destroy them, and not build them up." **Pslams28:5**

-----Give Thanks always-----

Thanks giving is a mystery of the kingdom that dismantles and conquers prevailing obstacle. We are commanded to give thanks always for this is the will of God in Christ Jesus concerning us. *"In every thing give thanks: for this is the will of God in Christ Jesus concerning you."* **1theo5:18**

Thus when we *"walk by the Spirit,"* we experience the fulfillment of this prophecy. The Holy Spirit produces in us desires for God's way that are stronger than our fleshly desires, and thus he causes us to walk in God's statutes.

Works of the Flesh and Fruit of the Spirit

-----Confess your sins-----

We all know that Jesus is Lord. You have to take time to confess it with your mouth.

-----Pray-----

"And he spake a parable unto them to this end, that men ought always to pray, and not to faint;"

"Pray without ceasing."

-----Trust in the Lord-----

We are told *"They that trust in the Lord shall be as mount Zion, which cannot be removed, but abideth for ever."* **Psalms 125:1**

Chapter 2 - How do we Walk by the Spirit?

CONCLUSION

"And almost all things are by the law purged with blood; and without shedding of blood is no remission." **Hebrews 9:22**

If we have not been giving thanks even in our prayers. we have not been living right. Thanksgiving must become a daily ritual for every believer.

"Therefore if any man be in Christ, he is a new creature: old things are passed away; behold, all things are become new." **2cor 5:17**

What must I do to determine my divine visitation?

To determine divine visitation you must be born again. The word says as many as received him, to them gave He power to become the sons of God. Even to them that believe on his name.

To qualify for divine visitation do the following sincerely;

1) Acknowledge that you are a sinner and that He died for you. **Rom3:23**.

2) Repent of your sins. **Acts 3:19, Luke13:5, 2Peter3:9**

3) Believe in your heart that Jesus died for your sin. **Romans10:10**

4) Confess Jesus as the Lord over your life. **Romans10:10, Acts2:21**

Now repeat this Prayer after me,

      Say Lord Jesus, I accept you today, as my Lord and my savior, forgive me of my sins wash me with your blood. Right now, I believe, I am sanctified, I am save, I am free, I am free from the Power of sin to serve the Lord Jesus. Thank you Lord for saving me. Amen. Congratulation: YOU ARE NOW A BORN AGAIN CHRISTIAN

CHAPTER 3
PRAYER OF SALVATION

"Neither is there salvation in any other: for there is none other name under heaven given among men, whereby we must be saved." **Acts 4:12**

This small book will make no sense if after all we have said about the blood of Jesus Christ. You have not confessed Him as your personal Lord and savior. All we have said from the beginning to this point will remain a mystery unless you give your life to Jesus Christ.

What must I do to determine my salvation?

To be saved we must be born again! The word says as many as received him, to them gave He power to become the sons of God. Even to them that believe on his name.

To qualify for divine visitation do the following sincerely;

1) Acknowledge that you are a sinner and that He died for you. **Rom 3:23**.

3) Believe in your heart that Jesus died for your sin. **Romans10:10**

4) Confess Jesus as the Lord over your life. **Romans10:10, Acts2:21**

Now repeat this Prayer after me,

Say Lord Jesus, I accept you today, as my Lord and my savior, forgive me of my sins wash me with your blood. Right now, I believe, I am sanctified, I am save, I am free, I am free from the Power of sin to serve the Lord Jesus. Thank you Lord for saving me.

AMEN

Join a bible believing church or you can join us proclaim the power of God in the gospel of Jesus Christ. There is Power in the blood of the lamb.

Chapter 3 - Prayer of Salvation

MIRACLE CARE OUTREACH

"...But that the members should have the same care one for another" **1cor12:25**

We are all members of the body of Christ. Jesus commanded us to love our neighbor as ourselves. This includes caring for one another as a member of one body. True love is expressed in caring and giving. The word says for God so Love He gave....

Reach out to someone in need of Jesus, help someone in crisis find Christ. Look out and prove your love to Jesus by caring and inviting your friends and associates to find Jesus the Healer.

Invite your friends to our Home Care Cell Fellowship (Miracle chapel Intl Satellite fellowship) In the USA at 33 Schley Street Newark New Jersey 07112.

If you are in Nigeria—**MIRACLE OF GOD MINISTRIES**

A.K.A "MIRACLE CHAPEL INTL"
Mpama –Egbu-Owerri Imo state Nigeria.

(Home Care Cell fellowship Group). We meet every Tuesday at 6:00pm-7:00pm.

LIFE IS NOT ALL ABOUT DURATION BUT ITS ALL ABOUT DONATION

What does the above statement mean?....

"Life consists not in accumulation of material wealth.." **Luke 12:15.**

"But it's all about liberality....meaning- what you can give and share with others." **Proverb 11:25.**

When you live for others--You live forever- because you out live your generation by the legacy you live behind after you depart into glory to be with the Lord. But when you live to yourself - you are reduced to self—you are easily forgotten when you die and depart in glory.

Permit me to admonish you today to live your life to be a blessing to a soul connected to you today.

Chapter 3 - Prayer of Salvation

I want you to know that so many souls are connected and looking up to you, and through you so many souls will be saved and rescued from destruction. Will you disciple someone today to find Jesus Christ?

"As a genuine Christian; it is your duty to evangelize Jesus Christ to all you meet on your way. Jesus is still in the healing business-Jesus is still doing miracles from time of old to now.

Therefore tell someone about Jesus Christ today, disciple and bring them to Church."

John 1:45 Philip findeth Nathanael....

Please to prove the sincerity of your love for God today; please become a soul winner. The dignity of your Christianity is hidden in your boldness to proclaim and evangelize Jesus Christ to all you meet on your way.

There is a question mark on the integrity of your Christianity until you become a life soul winner. Invite someone to join us worship the Lord Jesus this coming Sunday.

MIRACLE OF GOD MINISTRIES

PILLARS OF THE COMMISSION

We Believe, Preach and Practice the following,

1) We believe and preach Salvation to every living human being

2) We believe and preach Repentance and forgiveness of sins

3) We believe and preach the baptism of the Holy Spirit and Spiritual gifts

4) We believe and teach the Prosperity

5) We believe and preach Divine Healing and Miracles (Signs & Wonder)

6) We believe and preach Faith

7) We believe and Proclaim the Power of God (Supernatural)

8) We believe and Proclaim Praise & Worship to God

Chapter 3 - Prayer of Salvation

9) We believe and preach Wisdom

10) We believe and preach Holiness (Consecration)

11) We believe and preach Vision

12) We believe and teach the Word of God

13) We believe and teach Success

14) We believe and practice Prayer

15) We believe and teach Deliverance

This 15 stones form the Pillars of Our Commission.

Become part of this church family and follow this great move of God.

MY HEART FELT PRAYER FOR YOU

It is my prayer that you testify today about the goodness of the Lord. I desire for you to have an encounter with our Lord Jesus Christ.

Now let me Pray for you:

Heavenly father may today be a day of new beginning for this precious love one. Lord God of heaven open a new chapter in the life of this precious love one reading this book today. May all their prayers be answered in the mighty name of Jesus. We thank you Jesus for hearing us. In Jesus mighty name. **Amen**

Chapter 3 - Prayer of Salvation

*****Encounter with God******

Unless you are left alone you are not ready to encounter God. Jacob was left alone and he encountered God. I strongly urge you to create a quiet time with your God. A time of meditation and reflection. God is still omnipotent and all powerful. But you have to discover this by prayer and meditation in the word of God.

Jacob encountered God

"And Jacob was left alone; and there wrestled a man with him until the breaking of the day. And when he saw that he prevailed not against him, he touched the hollow of his thigh; and the hollow of Jacob's thigh was out of joint, as he wrestled with him. And he said, Let me go, for the day breaketh. And he said, I will not let thee go, except thou bless me. And he said unto him, What is thy name? And he said, Jacob. And he said, Thy name shall be called no more Jacob, but Israel: for as a prince hast thou power with God and with men, and hast prevailed." **Genesis32:24-28**.

Apostle Paul encountered God

"And as he journeyed, he came near Damascus: and suddenly there shined round about him a light from heaven: And he fell to the earth, and heard a voice saying unto him, Saul, Saul, why persecutest thou me? And he said, Who art thou, Lord? And the Lord said, I am Jesus whom thou persecutest: it is hard for thee to kick against the pricks." **Acts9:3-5**

CHAPTER 4
ABOUT THE AUTHOR

Rev Franklin N Abazie is the founding and Presiding Pastor of Miracle of God Ministries with headquarters in Newark, New Jersey USA and a branch church in Owerri- Imo State Nigeria. He is following the footsteps of one of his mentors, Oral Roberts (Healing Evangelist) of the blessed memory.

The Lord passed Oral Roberts healing mantle two days before he went to be with the Lord at age 91 into the hand of healing evangelist-Rev Franklin N Abazie in a vision.

In all his services the Power and Presence of God is present to heal all in his audience. He is an ordained man of God with a Healing Ministry reviving the healing and miracle ministry of Jesus Christ of Nazareth.

Pastor Franklin N Abazie, is called by God with a unique mandate:

"THE MOMENT IS DUE TO IMPACT YOUR WORLD THROUGH THE REVIVAL OF THE HEALING & MIRACLE MINISTRY OF JESUS CHRIST OF NAZARETH.

I AM SENDING YOU TO RESTORE HEALTH UNTO THEE AND I WILL HEAL THEE OF THY WOUNDS. SAID THE LORD OF HOST"

He is a gifted ardent Teacher of the word of God who operates also in the office of a Prophet, generating and attracting undeniable signs & wonders, special miracles and healings, with apostolic fireworks of the Holy Ghost.

He is the founding and presiding senior Pastor of this fast growing Healing ministry.

He has written over 86 inspirational, healing and transforming books covering almost all aspect of divine healing and life. He is happily married and blessed with children.

BOOKS BY REV FRANKLIN N ABAZIE

1) Commanding Abundance
2) The outcome of faith
3) Understanding the secret of prevailing prayers
4) Understanding the secret of the man God uses
5) Activating my due Season
6) Overcoming Divine Verdicts
7) The Outcome of Divine Wisdom
8) Understanding God's Restoration Mandate
9) Walking in the Victory and Authority of the truth
10) Gods Covenant Exemption
11) Destiny Restoration Pillars
12) Provoking Acceptable Praise
13) Understanding Divine Judgment
14) Activating Angelic Re-enforcement
15) Provoking Un-Merited Favor
16) The Benefits of the Speaking faith
17) Understanding Divine Arrangement

18) Understanding Divine Healing
19) The Mystery of Endurance
20) Obeying Divine Instructions
21) Understanding the Voice of God
22) Never give up on Hope
23) The prevailing Power of faith
24) Understanding Divine Prosperity
25) The Reward of Prayer
26) Covenant Keys to Answered Prayers
27) Activating the Forces of Vengeance
28) Put your faith to work
29) Where is your trust?
30) The Audacity of the Blood of Jesus
31) Redeeming Your Days
32) The force of Vision
33) Breaking the shackles of Family Curses
34) Wisdom for Marriage Stability
35) The winners Faith
36) The Prayer solution
37) The power of Prayer
38) The Effective Strategy of Prayer
39) The Prayer that Works
40) Walking in Forgiveness
41) ThePower of the Grace of God

42) The power of Persistence
43) Overcoming Divine verdicts
44) The audacity of the blood of Jesus.
45) The prevailing power of the blood of Jesus
46) The benefit of the speaking faith.
47) Fearless faith
48) Redeeming Your Days.
49) The Supernatural Power of Prophecy
50) The companionship of the Holy Spirit
51) Understanding Divine Judgement
52) Understanding Divine Prosperity
53) Dominating Controlling Forces
54) The winners Faith
55) Destiny Restoration Pillars
56) Developing Spiritual Muscles
57) Inexplicable faith
58) The lifestyle of Prayer
59) Developing a positive attitude in life.
60) The mystery of Divine supply
61) Encounter with God's Power
62) Walking in love
63) Praying in the Spirit
64) How to provoke your testimony

65) Walking in the reality of the Anointing
66) The reality of new birth
67) The price of freedom
68) The Supernatural power of faith
69) The Power of Persistence
70) The intellectual components of Redemption
71) Overcoming Fear
72) The Force of Vision
73) Overcoming Prevailing Challenges
74) The Power of the Grace of God
75) My life & Ministry
76) The Mystery of Praise

MIRACLE OF GOD MINISTRIES

NIGERIA CRUSADE 2012

MIRACLE OF GOD MINISTRIES

NIGERIA CRUSADE 2012

MIRACLE OF GOD MINISTRIES

NIGERIA CRUSADE

2012

MIRACLE
OF
GOD
MINISTRIES

NIGERIA CRUSADE

2012

www.ingramcontent.com/pod-product-compliance
Lightning Source LLC
Chambersburg PA
CBHW021134300426
44113CB00006B/424